# Heaven is Real

# A Diary of Visions and Hope

### Daryl J. Minor

To:
Sandy Martin,
May our Lord
and Savior Bless
you as you read
the contents of
this Book, and
May they bring
you ever closer to
Him.
Daryl J. M 1/17/15

*Heaven is Real, A Diary of Visions and Hope*
by Daryl J. Minor

Printed in the United States of America

ISBN 9781624198267

Unless otherwise indicated, Bible quotations are taken from the Holy Bible, New International Version (NIV). Copyright © 1967 by Biblica.

Contact Information:
Daryl J. Minor
P.O. Box 3396 McAllen, Texas 78502 USA
darylminor@yahoo.com

www.xulonpress.com

# Dedication

This book is dedicated first of all, to my Lord and Savior Jesus Christ, to our Pastors, Salome and Juanita Villarreal, who have been used by God to be a pillar of strength and encouragement to my family and myself throughout the years, to my wife Marcia, who has been an inspiration to me and the love of my life, to our two daughters Marcie and Darcy, who have brought countless moments of joy, love and happiness into our lives with each and every passing day, to our favorite dogs Como-Tu and Nancy who have shown what faithfulness and unconditional love is all about and to my father John Minor, who I admire and love dearly and who, by his very example has helped me to become the man I am today. I would also like to dedicate this book in memory of my mother Mary Ann Minor, my Aunt Sonia Atkinson, my grandmother Agnes Atkinson, my great grandmother Anne Overstreet, my father-in-law Celso Yerena, Sr., my mother-in-law Conchita Yerena, my brother-in-law Ruben Yerena, and my dear sister in Christ, Kathy Benson, of whom we all love and miss dearly, but by the grace of God have been called to be with Jesus in Heaven where they are all now safely home and all of which we will see again in Heaven one day.

# Table of Contents

# Introduction

*T*his book is about just some of the many true to life and factual experiences that other individuals and I have had since 1974, in regards to visions, stories of hope and most of all, about God's precious gift of eternal life that we all can have through his one and only son Jesus Christ our Lord. Also, it is my hope that after reading this book and the many passages of scripture from the Bible that are also included within it, that you will come to understand that we are indeed living in the last days right before Jesus returns for his Church, that Heaven and Hell do indeed exist and are very much real, that Jesus, the Holy Spirit, Angel's, the Devil and Demons are not made up, and that man does indeed have a soul that will feel, think and live forever once a person's body ceases to exist in this world of ours as we know it. However, most of all, I pray that your life will be touched and you will come to understand that in spite of all we go through on our pilgrimage through this Earth, that Jesus will always be there to help as well as save all of those who call upon his precious and wonderful name.

## The Day of the Lord

And afterward, I will pour out my Spirit on all people. Your sons and daughters will prophesy, your old men will dream dreams, your young men will see visions. Even on my servants, both men and women, I will pour out my Spirit in those days. I will show wonders in the heavens and on the earth, blood and fire and billows of smoke. The sun will be turned to darkness and the moon to blood before the coming of the great and dreadful day of the LORD. And everyone who calls on the name of the LORD will be saved; for on Mount Zion and in Jerusalem there will be deliverance, as the LORD has said, among the survivors whom the LORD calls (Joel 2:28-32).

# Chapter 1

# The Angel's Right Hand

It was around 1971 when I was only 14 years old, that my Father and Mother finally decided to move from New Haven, Michigan back to Cumberland, Wisconsin. You could say that the experience was rather thrilling, especially since not only would we be moving back to the town where I was born, I would finally be able to see my grandmother and my childhood friends that I grew up with once again as well. I would also be able to spend more time with them after living so far away for so many years. The day finally came that I dreaded and that was when I would have to go back to school. Oh well; I thought that I could take just about anything, but little did I know just how wrong I would be. There I was, just starting my first year in the 8th grade at Cumberland High School in Cumberland, Wisconsin. To be honest with you, it was rather scary at first, but soon I was able to get used to going to what I thought was a very big place on a daily basis after quite a short while. As time went on, I ran into a young man in the 8th grade named Herb Switzer. I did not know it then, but Herb was a born again Christian and the leader of the Morning Prayer group at our high school. He was also the leader of a local group in Cumberland, Wisconsin called Youth Alive for Christ (YAC).

Now, not knowing anything about Jesus myself at the time, I did not understand why Herb was continually being so nice to me, why he kept smiling at me when we would pass by each other in the hallways at school on our way to class, or why he kept saying, "God bless you" every time he saw me. However, as time went on, Herb began to ask me each time he would see me at school if I would like to go to Bible studies with him when I had the chance. In fact, another member of the youth group named Kathy Benson would also ask me the very same thing. Because I had a very bad temper and did not understand God's love, I basically told them both to buzz off and to just leave me alone from then on. That did not stop Herb or Kathy however, and in fact not only did they both continue to say "God bless you" to me every time they saw me in the hallways at school, they also convinced the other 50 or so members from the Christian youth group to also start smiling at me, saying "God bless you" and asking me if I would like to go to Bible studies every time they would all see me as well. By this time, it was finally beginning to annoy me so much that whenever I would see Herb, Kathy, or any of the other members from the youth group at school I would either run or hide until they were finally all gone.

Well, let me tell you, Herb and the other youth from the Bible Study group continued to be very persistent. They all kept right on smiling at me, and never stopped praying for me or gave up on me, especially in their efforts to talk to me about Jesus all through the entire time that I was in high school. It was during the time that I was in the 11th grade though, that would finally become the actual turning point in my life. The reason I say this is that as I entered the 11th grade, I started to become very depressed on a regular basis. I realized or thought that I did not have any hope and as the result of all of this, began to wonder what life was all about. I basically spent nearly my whole 11th grade year (1974) crying, staring in my bedroom mirror for hours on end at my own reflection, listening to music that was not very uplifting and also trying to figure out a reason just to live. While all of this was taking place in my life and unbeknownst to me at the time, Herb Switzer and the other youth from the YAC Bible Study group were still praying for me on a regular basis.

In fact, Herb told me about a year later that during March of 1974, he and around 50 or more youth from YAC all went to a prayer retreat that was located in Green Lake, Wisconsin. It was at this prayer retreat that they began to pray for me and many others in a prayer tower at the retreat. While they were all praying later on during the evening, a white dove apparently flew up in the midst of them and then left the prayer tower and continued to fly in the direction of my home that was located in Crystal Lake, Wisconsin at the time. Now I would like you to know that none of the other youth in the prayer tower, including Herb or Kathy, knew what was yet to happen later during the fall of that year. They did not know what would happen due to their obedience to the Lord and because they believed and asked the Lord with all their hearts by faith and not by sight for the salvation of my soul and the souls of many others that the Lord had laid upon their hearts to pray for. In regards to the power of prayer, the Bible says in Proverbs 15:29 that "the Lord hears the prayer of the righteous." In 2 Samuel 22:4,-7 David's prayer for deliverance was also heard: "I will call upon the Lord, *who is* worthy to be praised; so shall I be saved from my enemies. In my distress I called upon the Lord and cried out to my God; He heard my voice from His temple, and my cry *entered* his ears." The faithfulness of these young boys and girls in regards to praying for the souls of the lost, including my own, would indeed bring forth many miracles of salvation later on during the fall of 1974.

Now it was during the latter part of 1974 that I had not seen Herb or any of the other youth from the group for a while at school. This was because I was only going to school half days at the time. Once classes were finished, I would catch a ride on the bus to go back home each afternoon itself. Although my mother was home every day, I would just go upstairs to my room when I returned from school and spend the rest of the afternoon crying while staring at my own reflection in my bedroom mirror. During this time, I continued to wonder what life was all about and also contemplated if life itself was worth living. Then around November of 1974 I finally decided in my own foolish mind that life had no meaning or purpose and because of this, I started to plan just exactly how to go about ending my own life. Well December of 1974 finally came and then around the 15th of December I took a bottle of aspirin and some wine up to my room and lay down in my bed. When I was resting in my bed, I said to myself that this would be the day that all would finally end, but because I was so physically and mentally exhausted, I just fell into a deep sleep on my pillow instead. The next day on December 16th 1974 however, I was sure that this would be the day my life would end. On that day I did not go to school at all, but instead spent most of my time in my room. My mother was home, but as usual, she would be watching her soap operas downstairs in the living room while rocking in her favorite chair.

On this particular day that I was planning to take my life, I first went back downstairs and then into the living room where my mother was sitting. I then told her just how much I loved her and that she meant the world to me. Then as I went into the kitchen, I quickly glanced at the wall above the stove and noticed that the cuckoo clock said 11:45 A.M. I then went back to my bedroom upstairs, once again grabbed my bottle of aspirin and wine and proceeded to lie down sideways on my pillow. With my head and eyes filled with tears, I was looking at the bedroom door on the far north side of the room. I then closed my eyes for a short while and cried and cried, but then as I slowly opened my eyes, I saw something that was beyond description. In front of me was the brilliant, whitish colored right hand of an angel. The palm of the hand was open and was even with my head and about two feet in front of me and around 3 feet above the floor. I do recall very clearly that as soon as I saw this beautiful hand, I was no longer afraid, that my name did not matter, that time no longer had meaning and that I was engulfed in an endless and timeless sea of love, tranquility and peace of which I did not want to leave. I also remember that the hand of this angel was around three times the size of an ordinary man's hand. It was perfect in every way and the color of what we call white here was much different than the whiteness or brilliance of the hand itself.

As I continued to stare at the hand, I noticed that there was a garment or some type of clothing near the portion of what we would refer to as our wrist, so I knew that there was a very big angel kneeling right in front of me. For whatever reason, all that God wanted me to see was only the hand itself. Now as I continued to look at the angel's hand, I noticed that it had all the lifelines like we do on our palms. The hand then moved counter-clockwise very slowly and then suddenly stopped. As it was doing this, I noticed that it also had fingernails like we do, but they were perfect in shape and form. The hand itself was proportional in regards to form, size, and shape, or in other words, everything about it was without flaw of any kind. Now all the while that I am staring at this hand, I can hear someone talking to me inside; not through my ears did I hear, but it was as though I understood what was being said to me in my mind, heart and soul. The brightness of this angel's hand was like lightning, the beauty was utterly indescribable and as far as the color is concerned, it does not exist in our world in any way, shape or form. The love that I felt was a love like no other; it was a love that went through me deep into my mind, heart, soul and innermost being.

I remember the impression of what I was understanding

or being told and that was not to be afraid, that everything was going to be okay, that there was hope, that life was indeed worth living, that Jesus loved me very much, that he had a purpose for my life and that heaven was very much real. Being in a place where nothing else mattered except this immense love that had carried me away, I finally saw this angel's right hand slowly fade away from my sight. Once this happened, I then got up off my bed, kneeled down next to my bedroom window, and with my room being filled with so much love and peace, I bowed my head, folded my hands, and then asked Jesus to forgive me of all my sins, to come into my heart and to be the Lord and Savior of my life because I wanted to live with him forever in heaven. After I did this, I proceeded to go back downstairs and throw the aspirin and wine bottles away in the trash can. I noticed as I glanced once again back upon the wall that the clock said 1:00 P.M. It seemed that only moments before I had gone upstairs to end my life, but Jesus sent one of his big angels to fight for my soul and to save my life in the end.

This meant that although time no longer existed or had meaning when I saw the angel's hand in front of me, that I must have been visited for a least an hour or so, even though it only seemed that I had just walked upstairs a few moments earlier. I then went into the living room where my mother was sitting. Since she saw me smiling with a glow all over my face and a change that had just taken place inside me, she said, "Daryl what happened? It looks like you saw a ghost." I could not tell her though about the angel's hand that I just saw because for some reason I knew I was not supposed to at the time. Instead I knew that I needed to get a Bible, go to church and start praying for the salvation of my mother and the rest of my family from that moment on, just as Herb Switzer, Kathy Benson, and the rest of YAC prayed for me in the prayer tower during the beginning of 1974. Lastly, although there are no earthly words to describe what I saw, which would be just the first of many different types of visions and angel's that I would yet see in the years ahead, I will try to provide the following example of what the hand of the angel that I saw that day looked like.

Even though the color does not exist in this world, nor are the pictures perfect, just try to imagine the most perfect hand you could ever see, the purest and brightest white you could imagine, even more beautiful than a fresh Christmas snow fall or brighter than the brightest lightning and then maybe, just maybe, you will be able imagine just a little of what I saw. In doing so, I hope that the picture I have included will give you some type of an idea as to what I observed during that time.

# The Angel's Right Hand

# Chapter 2

# The Angel from Hell

*I*t was during the spring of 1975 when my father and mother decided to move from Crystal Lake, Wisconsin back into the town of Cumberland, Wisconsin, which of course was only around 6 or so miles away. I lived with my grandmother at her house for a while during that particular year, because the house my parents moved into did not have enough space for all of us at the time. While I was living with my grandmother at her house, I stayed upstairs in my own bedroom, which was very nice. My grandmother was a very special person and she loved the Lord very much as well. As far as her house was concerned, it was an older farm house and I enjoyed everything in regards to the way in which it was constructed, as well as how my grandmother had decorated each and every room. Since I just had to have a mirror in order to comb my hair, I really enjoyed the large antique mirror on the wall at the end of the stairs in the living room that was located on the first floor of the house.

In regards to this mirror and what would soon be taking place, it was on a Saturday afternoon during the spring of 1975. My Grandmother had just left the house to go to church with a dear friend of hers. I, on the other hand, had just finished showering upstairs and was getting ready to go to Bible studies with Herb Switzer, Kathy Benson, and the rest of the youth from YAC. I got dressed, then proceeded to go downstairs in order to comb my hair in front of my favorite mirror that was located in the living room. Now at the bottom of the staircase in my grandmother's living room, if you were to look to your left hand side you would see a very big double window located on the front east side. If you looked out the window and straight ahead you could see my great-grandmother's house located around 100 feet or so away. If you looked straight down, you would see two wooden doors that were open on each side, which were used to cover a deep opening to a stairs that lead to a basement right under the house itself. As far as what I was about to experience, it was not something that I was ever expecting, but for some reason I believe that the Lord allowed me to see as well as experience this for reasons that I did not understand at that time, but would in the future.

With my Bible tucked under my left arm, I proceeded to finish combing my hair in my favorite mirror. As soon as I was done, I then turned and started to walk towards the front door of the house that was located toward the north side of the living room. As I started to walk toward the front door, I felt as if someone or something was staring back at me through the window. Because of this feeling that I had, I stopped when I was in the center or about half way through the living room. I then, for some reason I do not yet know, turned first my head then my whole body towards the east in the direction of the big double window that was located in the center of the living room. The reason I stopped was because I was actually looking at a very big angel from hell, which was sort of standing or hovering right above the open basement doors on the outside of my great-grandmother's house, directly in my view as I looked out of the living room window. The angel appeared to be standing or hovering right in front or at the edge of some sort of very long, deep, dark and very big square-shaped tunnel. The tunnel itself was around 20 feet tall and 20 feet wide on each side, and slanted far down into the earth at about a 45-degree angle for what seemed to be a few miles or so.

In regards to this angel from hell that I was observing, I would like you to understand that I was not at all scared or frightened in the least. This was due to the great peace that I felt inside during the entire time I was observing the angel and that peace came from Jesus as well as the Holy Spirit. As I continued to observe just the features of the angel, the first thing I noticed was that its arms were folded inwards and down; its hands and fingers were all withered, curled up and also folded inward as if it had some type of sickness or disease. The color of the angel was not like the color of black we have here on this earth. The type of blackness that I saw is very hard to describe, since it was extremely dark and consisted of a kind of blackish-grey kind of color as well. The angel appeared to have male features by the shape or structure of its face, was around 12 or so feet tall and was proportional in regards to height, shape and form, except for the deformities that were evident upon its hands, fingers, face and body. It also wore a very long robe-like garment that consisted of a variety of different types of textures and shapes; of which looked very antique or old as well. The angel had two humps that were located behind its back, which appeared to include two very large and long wings, which were folded inwards and down behind its back on each side.

As I looked at the face of this angel, I noticed that the eyes were even darker than the darkness of the angel, which did not appear to have retinas like we do, because where the retinas should be there was only some type of great blackness inside them. In addition, as I gazed even deeper into the angel's eyes, I was also able to detect some type of extreme or unbearable hopelessness and a sense of complete alienation or isolation as well. As far as the mouth, nose, ears, eyebrows and hair, these were also even much darker in color than the rest of the angel's face or what I refer to as some type of lost spiritual body itself. In regards to other features this angel had, it seemed to have short hair that was parted in the middle and that was sort of matted downwards as if very dirty or something. It did not consist of any type of color as we know it, but the color of extreme darkness itself. Now as I continued to look at the angel, I was also looking at the tunnel it was standing or hovering in. The tunnel itself was also a very dark blackish grayish kind of color as well. What I especially remember about this tunnel is that there was not even a speck of light anywhere at all, not even the size of the tip of a needle or a grain of sand. The light we know and see on this earth even on the darkest of days, which still has some type of light, did not exist at all in this place for there was no such thing as light over there.

The tunnel itself seemed to also have some type of darkish grey color and a density to it as if everything, including the darkness in the tunnel where the angel was standing, was somehow moving or floating. It was compressed or compacted together with some kind of immense force or pressure upon it and looked as if it was located in some type of dimension where time, space and distance did not matter or apply as we know it to be within our world. As I continued to study this angel, after a while it finally realized that I was observing it. Once it did this, it seemed to be somehow very curious or surprised and shocked that I could actually see it. At this point, its eyes then seemed to open up and become much bigger. Then it began to slowly move its head and body towards me. When it started to do this, I then raised my right hand in the air, pointed it in the direction of the angel and said in a very firm voice, "In Jesus's name I cast you back to the pits of hell where you came from." Upon my saying these very words, the angel then suddenly opened its eyes and mouth as if in great fear and terror. I also noticed at this point that it appeared to be screaming and in shock by the shape of its mouth, eyes and other facial expressions, but I could not hear it with my own ears. The angel then started to descend backwards down, down, down, into the tunnel of blackness from which it came while still staring back at me the whole time. It was as if an immense and powerful force or being had bound its body, hands and arms with some type of cord or chain that I could not see with my eyes, then took it back to the pits of hell, by force whether it wanted to go there or not. Now as the angel was making its descent back into hell, this very big doorway opened up behind it. As this doorway swung fully open on both sides, I saw an even greater blackness which was blacker than the black of the tunnel located directly behind where the angel was headed. The blackness that I saw was like a sea or lake of immense and endless darkness. It had some type of great thickness to it and consisted of various shadows, shapes, objects and forms, all of which appeared to be moving up and down as well as hanging on to or clinging to each other as if not wanting or being able to let go out of fear. As the angel finally reached the end of the tunnel, it went into and through the other side of this doorway, then into what lied on the other side, to what I refer to as a sea of endless darkness. Once the angel was on the other side of the doorway, the doorway then slowly closed inwards from both sides. As the door closed, I saw what appeared to be very old, large, thick and wide wood-like planks running up, down and sideways across the door in all directions. In addition, I noticed that there was no doorknob or keyhole anywhere on this door, so in essence, whatever goes in stays in. Once in, there is no way to get out, since this door cannot be opened from or closed from either side. Finally, as I finished observing the tunnel, the door itself, the angel from hell, and the endless sea of darkness, the tunnel slowly vanished before my eyes. Once this happened, I sat down for a while and prayed, thought about what I had just seen, then went on to Bible studies.

Now as the years have gone by I have thought a lot about the reality of hell, the darkness and the keyless door I saw with no handle or doorknob attached. In regards to the darkness, the Bible says in Matthew 22:12-13, "And he saith unto him, 'Friend, how camest Thou in hither not having a wedding garment?' And he was speechless. Then said the king to the servants, 'Bind him hand and foot, and take him away, and cast him into outer darkness; there shall be weeping and gnashing of teeth". This may be a good description of the darkness that I saw, which in this case as the Bible says is outer-darkness, or darker than dark. As far as the door with no key, the Bible says in Revelation 1:18 that Jesus died, but he is now alive until the Ages of the Ages and that he has the keys of the gates of Death and of Hades! That would explain why there is no way to get into hell, no way to get out of hell and why there is no key hole or doorknob located anywhere on the doorway to hell. Jesus holds the very keys to the gates of hell and is the only one that can open or close the doorway or gates to hell itself. Lastly, as far as the reality of hell is concerned:

- It was designed originally for Satan and his demons (Matthew 25:41; Revelation 20:10).
- Hell is also a place of conscious torment, a furnace of fire where there will be weeping and gnashing of teeth (Matthew 13:50).
- It is a place where their worm does not die, and the fire is not quenched (Mark 9:48).
- Hell is also eternal and irreversible, a place where "the smoke of their torment goes up forever and ever and they have no rest day and night" (Revelation 14:11).
- However, God doesn't send people to hell; they choose it (Romans 1:18, 21, 25) and even those who

haven't heard of Christ are accountable for God's revelation in nature (Romans 1:20).

However, the mercy of Jesus who died for us on the cross gives all hope who ask for it, in that God will seek those who seek Him (Matthew 7:7; Luke 19:10). God has also provided the way of salvation to all (John 3:16, 17; 2 Corinthians 5:14, 15; 1 Timothy 2:6; 4:10; Titus 2:11; and 2 Peter 3:9). In the end, what I saw in regards to this angel from hell, a doorway to hell, the gates of hell and a glimpse of what lies beyond in regards to what I refer to as a sea of endless darkness, was very much real. This constitutes all the more reason to think twice about where one wishes to spend eternity. The following pictures are sort of what I saw in regards to the visions described in this chapter, but remember, these are only pictures and since there is no way to describe, to draw, or to match the colors of what I saw, these pictures hopefully will have to do.

# The Angel from Hell

# The Tunnel to Hell

# The Fires of Hell

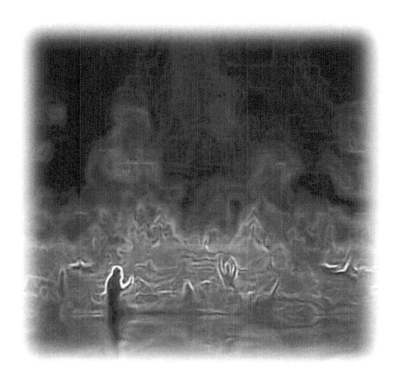

# Chapter 3

# The Angel from Heaven

*⊙∮∮~*

*D*uring the year of 1977, I lived in Rice Lake, Wisconsin along with four other Christian brothers of mine in a two story house that was located on 314 Noble Avenue. One of my Christian brothers was named Steve; he and I would go to a non-denominational church at a Bible school in Weyerhaeuser, Wisconsin. It was about 20 miles from where we lived. This particular church was a very special place and consisted of a discipleship training school that was run by Pastors Bill and Lou Lemke during that particular time. One Sunday morning during the summer of 1977 we arrived at church and began to pray while waiting for services to begin. After worshiping the Lord and before the sermon that Pastor Bill Lemke would soon be giving, we were all asked to sit for a while in order to enjoy some very beautiful singing from the choir of the Bible school's student music ministry. I remember very clearly that as the choir continued, everyone stood up and began to worship the Lord together. As I was standing, I closed my eyes for a while to pray and to continue to sing songs of worship to the Lord along with the other members of the church. Upon opening my eyes, I turned to look in the direction where the student choir was standing, specifically the center of the group.

It was at that time when I was observing a young man singing a solo that I noticed an angel from Heaven standing right in the middle of the group towards the center, right behind this young man in an open space. As I was looking at this angel from heaven, I first noticed that it had characteristics of the female gender. I could tell this due to the shape and formation of the face and the way in which the hair was colored, as well as situated on the angel's head. I also observed that this angel was around 6 feet tall, was very beautiful, had very short blondish colored hair that was parted in the middle on the top of her head and that consisted of many small curls, which were perfectly set in place. Now as I looked upon her face, I noticed that she had ears, a mouth, lips, a nose, eyebrows and eyes. Her face seemed to have some type of indescribable and beautiful color or complexion to it as well. In regards to her eyes in particular, she did not have retinas like we have, instead they appeared to be very bright like snow or as if there was lightning or some kind of great power with movement coming from within her eyes. She wore a long white gown that was not the color of white as we know it, but like a pure type of very beautiful white that was brighter than that of a freshly fallen snow. The robe she wore also had some type of gold colored belt attached around the middle, and her arms and hands were folded inwards and down in front of her.

I also noticed what appeared to be two areas that were located on both the left and right sides of her back, which appeared to be wings that were folded downwards towards the right and left sides of her shoulders, to the point where they almost touched the ground behind her. As I continued to stare at her, this female angel slowly turned her head towards me and looked straight into my eyes. When she did this, she began to tell me not to be scared, but her mouth was not moving. She was speaking into my thoughts without talking and somehow I was able to understand what she was saying.

She told me not to tell anyone what I saw until later in the future and that I would know the time in which to do so. In regards to her eyes once again, as she continued to look directly into my eyes, it was as though two separate beams of light like very bright and powerful spotlights had projected themselves outward from within each of her eyes and into my very eyes themselves. I also noticed during this time that her eyes were brighter and whiter than the white robe she was wearing. As I continued to look into her eyes, I saw what appeared to be some great force or power that was causing some type of movement within her eyes.

She was also perfect in every way, without flaw, was proportional and perfectly balanced as well. In addition, although she appeared to be of the female gender in regards to her appearance, posture, shape and form, I now understand from what I observed that there are both male and female angels due to the types of outward features and characteristics that each one displays. Finally, after around 20 minutes or so, the angel slowly faded away from my sight. In regards to my descriptions of this angel from heaven, it is very hard to depict or describe exactly what I observed, because the type of colors and the actual characteristics of the angel that I saw do not exist on this earth. To try to give you an idea however, I have attached a picture of what the female angel I saw looked like more or less, which cannot be compared in any way to exactly what I saw, but is only meant to give you sort of an idea as to what I observed. Lastly, I would like to include the following scriptures from the Bible that will help to describe what I saw and give you an idea as to what angels look like, what their eyes look like and why angels are here. In doing so, I hope you will realize that angels from heaven are indeed very much real.

In regards to what angels look like, this can be seen in the following Bible verses that touch upon this very subject. These Bible verses include:

- Matthew 28:2-4
  "His countenance was like lightning, and his raiment white as snow."

- Daniel 10:5-6 (KJV).
  "Then I lifted up mine eyes, and looked, and behold, a certain man clothed in linen, whose loins were girded with fine gold of Uphaz: His body also was like the beryl, and his face as the appearance of lightning, and his eyes as lamps of fire, and his arms and his feet like in color to polished brass, and the voice of his words like the voice of a multitude."

In regards to the purpose of angels, the Bible says that they are:

- vast in number (Hebrews 12:22; Revelation 5:11).
- they do not die (Luke 20:36).
- they are spirit beings (Hebrews 1:14).
- they are without bodies (Luke 24:39).
- they can assume bodily shape as people (Genesis 19:1-5).
- there is gender among them (Zechariah 5:9-11).
- they are wise, powerful, have personalities, are moral beings, are superior to people, but vastly inferior to God (2 Samuel 14:20; 2 Peter 2:11; Mark 8:38; 1 Peter 3:22; Hebrews 16).

God has also given us angels for the purpose of:

- Protecting – Keeping God's people out of physical danger, as in the cases of Daniel and the lions and his three friends in the fiery furnace (Daniel 3 and 6).
- Delivering – Getting God's people out of danger once they're in it. Angels released the apostles from prison in Acts 5 and repeated the process for Peter in Acts 12.

- Strengthening and encouraging – Angels strengthened Jesus after His temptation (Matthew 4:11), encouraged the apostles to keep preaching after releasing them from prison (Acts 5:19-20), and told Paul that everyone on his ship would survive the impending shipwreck (Acts 27:23-25).

- Answering prayer – God often uses angels as His means of answering the prayers of His people (Daniel 9:20-24; 10:10-12; Acts 12:1-17).

- Caring for believers at the moment of death – in the story of Lazarus and the rich man, we also read that angels carried the spirit of Lazarus to "Abraham's bosom" when he died (Luke 16:22).

In regards to the angel that I saw during this time, I would like you to view the following picture and although imperfect in its shape, coloration and form, I hope that it may give you some sort of an idea as to what I observed in regards to the angel from Heaven that is described in this chapter.

# The Angel from Heaven

# Chapter 4

# Visions of the Rapture

During the summer of 1978, I was still living in the same house along with the four Christian brothers of mine in the town of Rice Lake, Wisconsin. It was, I believe to be, during the month of June of this year that this particular vision occurred. Now the bedroom where I stayed and called my own was on the second story of our 2 bedroom house and I had the honor of sleeping on the top of a bunk bed. I believe that on the particular day that I had this vision it was around 3:00 A.M. It was during this time that I began to feel an immense peace sweep over my whole being and even though I was still in a very deep type of sleep physically, it was as if my spirit was wide awake and was observing through my own eyes all that was occurring, as well as what was going on all around me. Now since I was laying on my back with my head facing the ceiling of my bedroom on the upper part of the bunk bed I was sleeping on, the first thing that I observed was my whole body going upward off my bed at a very fast rate towards the ceiling within my bedroom. As this occurred, I remember that I looked down for a few moments back toward the bed below that I had just been sleeping on and realized that my physical body was no longer there.

As I continued to move toward the ceiling in my bedroom,

I saw the walls in my bedroom near my bed quickly pass underneath me as I finally began to approach the very top portion of the ceiling. Now around the time that my whole body felt like it was just about to pass through the top of the ceiling, my body at that moment quickly flew back down and I found myself laying on my back upon my bed looking upward at the ceiling once again. As soon as this occurred I then woke up from this deep sleep and also from the vision that I had just experienced during this time. I realized that although my body was asleep, my soul was very much awake and I knew that all I was experiencing and observing was very much real, was not a dream, and was as if I was totally aware of everything that was going on around me. I also believe that what I felt was just a hint of what will occur when Jesus finally returns for his body of believers or church during the rapture. This was the very reason that the Lord allowed me to experience as well as see this particular type of vision during this time.

In regards to a scriptural explanation of what the rapture is, the Bible explains more about this in the following scriptures:

> Listen, I tell you a mystery: We will not all sleep, but we will all be changed- in a flash, in the twinkling of an eye, at the last trumpet. "For the trumpet will sound, the dead will be raised imperishable, and we will be changed. For the perishable must clothe itself with the imperishable, and the mortal with immortality" (1 Corinthians 15:51-53).

Other scriptures that explain more about the rapture include 1 Thessalonians 4:13-17:

> Brothers, we do not want you to be ignorant about those who fall asleep, or to grieve like the rest of men,

who have no hope. We believe that Jesus died and rose again and so we believe that God will bring with Jesus those who have fallen asleep in him. According to the Lord's own word, we tell you that we who are still alive, who are left till the coming of the Lord, will certainly not precede those who have fallen asleep. For the Lord himself will come down from heaven, with a loud command, with the voice of the archangel and with the trumpet call of God, and the dead in Christ will rise first. After that, we who are still alive and are left will be caught up together with them in the clouds to meet the Lord in the air. And so we will be with the Lord forever.

Now I believe that the vision I saw was very much real and I was allowed to experience as well as see this, since Jesus wanted me to know that he is coming back very soon and to be prepared. I also believe that the Lord wanted me to tell others that he is coming very soon as well. In regards to Jesus's return for the church, this can also be seen in regards to scriptures that point to us living in the last days, which include Luke 17:22-37.

The days will come when you will long to see one of the days of the Son of Man, and you will not see it. They will say to you, "Look there! Look here!" Do not go away, and do not run after them. For just like the lightning, when it flashes out of one part of the sky, shines to the other part of the sky, so will the Son of Man be in His day. But first He must suffer many things and be rejected by this generation. And just as it happened in the days of Noah, so it will be also in the days of the Son of Man: they were eating, they were drinking, they were marrying, they were being given in marriage, until the day that Noah entered the ark, and the flood came and destroyed them all.

It was the same as happened in the days of Lot: they were eating, they were drinking, and they were buying, they were selling, they were planting, and they were Building; but on the day that Lot went out from Sodom it rained fire and brimstone from heaven and destroyed them all. It will also be just the same on the day that the Son of Man is revealed. On that day, the one who is on the housetop and whose goods are in the house must not go down to take them out; and likewise the one who is in the field must not turn back. Remember Lot's wife. Whoever seeks to keep his life will lose it, and whoever loses his life will preserve it. I tell you, on that night there will be two in one bed; one will be taken and the other will be left.

There will be two women grinding at the same place; one will be taken and the other will be left. Two men will be in the field; one will be taken and the other will be left. And answering they said to Him, "Where, Lord?" And he said to them, "Where the body is, there also the vultures will be gathered."

Finally, I would like to share with you in the following pictures, which are just some of the many examples of what the rapture may actually look like when it finally takes place. I will see you here, there or with Jesus in the air. Amen!

# The Rapture

# The Rapture

# Chapter 5

# Singing in Heavenly Tongues

*ꙮ*

Now it was around September or October of 1978. During this time I was living in Rice Lake, Wisconsin with five Christian brothers in a two story house. In regards to this particular experience that I had, it occurred around 2:00 A.M. My bedroom was still located on the second floor of the house and my bed was located at the top of a bunk bed. As I look back on this experience and what took place, I often think about what Heaven will be like and the types of sounds that we will all hear one day as we sing praises to the Lord. As far as the beautiful and indescribable experience that I would soon be blessed with, it occurred during the early morning hours on a Sunday, which was the same day that we all would soon be going to church. I recall getting ready for bed and then climbing up to the top of the bunk bed where I was to sleep that night. As soon as I lay down in my bed I leaned forward to say goodnight to my dear friend Pat who lay on the bottom bunk below me, then proceeded to say a prayer before actually falling off to sleep on my back. I recall suddenly waking up from my sleep and hearing the most beautiful singing coming from somewhere in the room. It was a sound that I had never heard with my own ears before, a combination of different types of pitches and levels that did not exist anywhere in this world of ours as we know it.

As I was looking around and trying to determine where this beautiful singing was coming from, I finally realized that my mouth was moving all on its own and that out of my own mouth the most beautiful singing and tones also emerged. I was not scared at all when this happened, but was rather peaceful. I then proceeded to cross my eyes as I was still lying down on my bed so that both eyes were looking towards my nose. I did this in order to see and confirm that my mouth was indeed moving on its own and that it was not being controlled by me, but rather by the Holy Spirit. I then continued to listen as my mouth sang in this beautiful, heavenly voice for a few more minutes until the wonderful singing slowly stopped. Once this had happened, I then looked back down to where my friend was sleeping below me. I did this to see if I had awakened him, but he was snoring and was still fast asleep as usual. The Bible teaches us that this is called speaking in tongues. In regards to speaking in tongues:

> Paul said, "John's baptism was a baptism of repentance. He told the people to believe in the one coming after him, that is, in Jesus." On hearing this, they were baptized into the name of the Lord Jesus. When Paul placed his hands on them, the Holy Spirit came on them, and they spoke in tongues and prophesied (Acts 19:4-6).

"They saw what seemed to be tongues of fire that separated and came to rest on each of them. All of them were also filled with the Holy Spirit and began to speak in other tongues as the Spirit enabled them" (Acts 2:3-4). In this case though, my spirit was actually singing in tongues to God through my mouth. As far as what was being said, I do not know, but the Bible teaches that "the Spirit itself maketh intercession for us with groanings which cannot be uttered" (Romans 8:26,

KJV). Lastly, does this mean that one will not go to Heaven, is not a Christian, or does not have Jesus in their hearts if they cannot speak in tongues? Of course not, for every Christian or true believer has already received the Holy Spirit once they asked Jesus into their hearts and can still go to Heaven without having to speak in tongues. The gift of tongues is a gift that all Christians can freely receive just by asking. The Bible also says the following:

> Now to each one the manifestation of the Spirit is given for the common good. To one there is given through the Spirit the message of wisdom, to another the message of knowledge by means of the same Spirit, to another faith by the same Spirit, to another the gifts of healing by that one Spirit, to another miraculous powers, to another prophecy, to another distinguishing between spirits, to another speaking in different kinds of tongues, and to still another interpretation of tongues. All these are the work of one and the same Spirit, and he gives them to each one, just as he determines (1 Corinthians 12:7-11).

In the end, Jesus has given to all those who call on his name many different types of spiritual gifts through the Holy Spirit. All a Christian needs to do is to ask and continue to always believe in regards to the types of gifts that the Lord has for them. If they do so, he will take care of everything else in his perfect time and place. As far as the Holy Spirit is concerned, I have included a picture of a dove, which is typically used in the Bible as an example or depiction of the Holy Spirit.

# The Holy Spirit

# Chapter 6

# My Mother's Salvation

*ᐞᔕᔕ~*

*T*first started to pray for my mother, father, brothers, sisters and aunts and uncles back in 1974, when I saw the vision of the angel I spoke of in the first chapter and at which time I asked Jesus into my heart. It was at that very time that Jesus laid upon my heart to start to lift my family up in prayer on a daily basis and to also believe with all my heart for their salvation. Now the Bible says that "the effectual fervent prayer of a righteous man availeth much" (James 5:16). Also in Acts 16:13 it says, "Believe on the Lord Jesus, and you and your family will be saved." For the next 13 years and even as I still do to this very day, I began to pray and talk to my family, aunts, uncles, grandmother, grandfather, cousins and every person I saw about God's plan of salvation. It is very simple and states that "if you confess with your mouth, 'Jesus is Lord,' and believe in your heart that God raised him from the dead, you will be saved" (Romans 10:9, KJV). As I continued to be faithful in my prayers, the Lord spoke to me about Abraham from the Bible.

Abraham had a nephew named Lot, who also had a wife and sons; they all lived in a very wicked city called Sodom and Gomorrah. Now these cities were about to be destroyed for their wickedness, but Abraham (even though he lived far away) prayed to God in Genesis 18:16-33 the following prayer:

Will you indeed sweep away the righteous with the wicked? Suppose there are fifty righteous within the city; will you sweep away the place and not forgive it for the fifty righteous who are in it? Far be it from you to do such a thing, to slay the righteous with the wicked, so that the righteous fare as the wicked! Far be that from you! Shall not the Judge of all the earth do what is just?,(NJKV).

Now God did indeed hear Abraham's prayer. It was because of Abraham's continued persistence and faith in believing that God would indeed hear his prayer and save Lot and his family in spite of his not knowing when, how, or even with whom that made all the difference. Abraham just prayed a prayer of faith and believed that God would take care of the rest. You could say that God has called us all to be Abrahams, in that we too, are to pray in spite of not even knowing how God will save someone we love.

To provide a financial miracle, to heal a health condition, or for whatever the reason, God wants us to be persistent in our prayers. We are to never give up and most of all to believe, even though we may not see the actual outcome of our prayers, or the method God chooses to answer our prayer until later. In this case, through Abraham's prayers of faith, God sent angels to provide the escape and the way to salvation. In regards to my own family, it was sometime during the year of 1983 that my mother was told she had stomach cancer. I, of course, lived in Texas, which was well over 2,000 miles away. As I spoke to my mother on the phone, I talked to her about Jesus and God's plan of salvation, as well as letting her know that she was in my prayers. Now my very first thought was, "How could I possibly save her?" The Lord spoke to me and told me to pray like Abraham and that he would take care of the rest, so I continued to pray for my mom especially. During the summer of 1987 two very special things happened. The first thing my mother told me about was a true story of what had happened to her that June. Apparently, my parents took a weekend camping trip to Cumberland, Wisconsin to a place called Eagles Point. Now as my mother told it to me, she explained that she went down to the shore to sit for a while and put her feet in the water.

As she was doing this, another women from Minnesota sat right down next to my mother. She began to tell my mother that the Lord told her and her husband to come to this place that they have never been and to look for a lady with short blond hair sitting on a lake by the shore with her feet in the water. She then did what she was told, found my mother sitting by the shore and began to tell her about Jesus. She then went to see her husband, who then took my father fishing and also began telling my father about Jesus as well. You could say that God did indeed hear my prayers after 13 years and brought a couple from Minnesota to plant the seeds of salvation within the hearts of both my parents. However, that was only the beginning. It was during the month of July after visiting with my family in Cameron, Wisconsin that I was actually planning on returning to Edinburg, Texas in order to finish up my studies at the University of Texas Pan American. On this particular day in July however, my mom and I were alone in the house and you could feel a great peace that set upon the entire house. I then went into the living room next to my mother, who was sitting on her favorite rocking chair and started to talk to her about Jesus and God's plan of salvation through his son.

It was then that my mom, who was very frail and weak at the time due to cancer, looked at me with her big, blue eyes and said, "Daryl, I would like to live forever with Jesus in Heaven and would like to ask him in my heart." There we were, my mother and I, after 13 years of faithful prayer. We finally both knelt down together on the living room floor on that bright, sunny day in July of 1987 and as we did, my mother asked Jesus to come into her heart and to become the Lord and Savior of her soul and life. She did so by repeating the following prayer which states: "Dear God in heaven, I come to you in the name of Jesus. I acknowledge to you that I am a sinner; I am sorry for my sins and the life that I have lived; I need your forgiveness. I believe that your only begotten Son Jesus Christ shed His precious blood on the cross at Calvary and died for my sins. I am now willing to turn from my sin." You said in your Holy Word, Romans 10:9 "That if thou shalt confess with thy mouth the Lord Jesus, and shalt believe in thine heart that God hath raised him from the dead, thou shalt be saved". Right now I confess Jesus as the Lord of my life. With my whole heart, I believe that God raised Jesus from the dead. This very moment I accept Jesus Christ as my own personal Savior and according to His Word, right now I am saved. Jesus I also thank you for your unlimited grace which has saved me from all of my sins and for dying for me on the cross and giving me eternal life. Amen."

It was at that point that my mother looked up at me with tears of extreme happiness running down her face from her big, blue eyes. Her face was also full of joy and peace as well. She then looked directly into my eyes and said, "Daryl, my son, I am not scared anymore. I feel so much peace inside. I know that I belong to Jesus now and that everything is going to be okay." We then got up from the floor where we had been kneeling and prayed some more. We continued to pray every day and talk about scriptures from the Bible as well. As time passed, I finally left for Texas in August of 1987 to resume my studies, but never stopped praying for my mother. After a few months passed, I received a phone call during October from the Rice Lake Regional Hospital of Rice Lake, Wisconsin.

They informed me that they had just picked my mother up from her home and that she had less than a day to live. I called her that same day and my father put the phone up to her ear. I went on to tell my mother just how much I loved her, but most of all talked more about Jesus and asked her again if she knew where she was going. My mother with her last breaths said "Daryl, I love you very much. Son, I don't want you to worry, because I am no longer in pain and I am going to be with Jesus. I am going home." With those very last words my mother was ushered into the gates of Heaven by her guardian angels to be with Jesus forever more.

I was indeed sad at that time because my dear mother had left this earth, but I was also happy knowing that she was safely home and that I would also see her again one day very soon. As far as my father, brothers, sisters, aunts, uncles, cousins, friends and people that I meet on a daily basis are concerned, I never stop praying for them. I always talk to them about Jesus, believe that they will be saved too, and that God will decide just how, when and where that will actually happen. The only thing I needed to do was just keep praying and believing, and to give them all to God as well as trust that Jesus through the Holy Spirit would take care of all the rest. Amen and Amen! Lastly, please see the following picture and poem that I have dedicated in loving memory of my mother Mary Ann Minor.

# Going to be with Jesus

# Poem # 1
# Home in Heaven

I am home in Heaven, dear ones;
Oh, so happy and so bright!
There is perfect joy and beauty
In this everlasting light. All the pain and grief is over,
Every restless tossing passed;
I am now at peace forever,
Safely home in Heaven at last. Did you wonder I so calmly
Trod the valley of the shade?
Oh! but Jesus's love illumined
Every dark and fearful glade. And He came Himself to meet me
In that way so hard to tread;
And with Jesus's arm to lean on,
Could I have one doubt or dread? Then you must not grieve
so sorely,
For I love you dearly still:
Try to look beyond earth's shadows,
Pray to trust our Father's will. There is work still waiting for you,
So you must not idly stand;
Do it now, while life remaineth-
You shall rest in Jesus' land. When that work is all completed,
He will gently call you Home;
Oh, the rapture of that meeting,
**Oh, the joy to see you come!**

# Chapter 7

# The Angels Sang from Heaven

*T*met my soon to be wife Marcia during the summer of 1987. I was introduced to her by her younger sister Connie at the University of Texas Pan American in Edinburg, Texas in a math class that both of us attended at the time. Now the day finally arrived when I called her for the very first time on the phone. When I did, I asked her if I could go to her house in order to meet her as well as the rest of her family in person. I remember that after she said yes, I quickly hopped into my car and headed towards her house itself as fast as I could go. As soon as I realized I was almost there, I suddenly became really nervous and worried if everyone, especially Marcia, would actually like me. Well to my surprise, once I stepped through the front door of their house, I was immediately accepted as part of the family by her father Celso Yerena, Sr., her mother Conchita Garcia de Yerena, the rest of her brothers and sisters, but most of all by Marcia herself. I think that Marcia's father especially liked me though and the reason being that we both had very long mustaches at the time.

During this first visit to Marcia's house, her mother asked me to sit at the table for something to eat. As soon as I sat down, I was immediately served a very big glass of freshly made lemonade and some very delicious tacos as well. While I was eating, I began to choke on the lemonade, the reason being that I must have been drinking it much too fast. As I was choking, I noticed that Marcia started to cry due to her worrying over my condition. It was then at that very moment that the Lord showed me the beauty of my future wife's heart and said that she would be the one I would marry later on. Well, I soon stopped choking and as the months passed I asked Marcia if she would like to be my girlfriend, and later after a while my fiancé. As we got to know each other more, we would spend a lot of time at church with her mother and father. We also went to Mexico and other places. Marcia's mother and father were very special people. They both loved the Lord very much, were full of wisdom and most of all knew how to laugh, love and live. Most of the time that Marcia's parents and I were together, we would laugh and joke around in the right way and always sought to look at the simple things in life. It was during the latter part of 1987 that I finally asked Marcia to marry me. We were married on February 12, 1988 at Liberty Temple Church in Pharr, Texas.

Although this was a very joyous occasion, Marcia's mother could not come to the wedding ceremony due to her being very ill at the time. Well, we got married that day and I have always thanked the Lord for bringing my wife Marcia into my life. Now my mother-in-law, Conchita, continued to become worse off in regards to her health condition. As time went on, my father-in-law Celso Sr., my wife and I took her to a hospital that was located in Monterrey N.L., Mexico. During the months ahead, my wife, her father and I would continue to make the long drive to visit her in Mexico every week. During one of our visits in June of that year, I approached the bed where my mother-in-law Conchita was laying down on. I could see that she had both of her arms extended in the air, was looking up towards heaven with her eyes open and was praying and singing as well. As I came next to her bed, she took my hand and looked into my eyes. Although she could not speak, I knew she was telling me that everything was going to be okay, to take care of her daughter, that she loved me, she was happy I had married her daughter, and most of all that she would soon be going home to be with Jesus. She was also praying for her daughter Marcia. As my wife went next to her bed where her mother was, her mother put her hand on Marcia's stomach, then looked at her and smiled. We did not know it yet, but my wife Marcia was pregnant with our first daughter Marcie at the time.

As the day went on and after spending time with Marcia's mother, we all went down stairs to the first floor of the hospital in order to find the best place to rest for the night. We finally found some chairs lined up against a wall near a door on the first floor of the hospital, which was out of the way and offered some privacy as well. The only thing that we noticed was that there was a big air vent near where we were sitting, but that did not seem to matter much, especially since we were all very tired. Keep in mind before I explain what happened next, that no radios or music was allowed in the hospital at all. In fact, loud noises and talking were also prohibited as well. This was done in order to ensure that all patients could get the proper rest that they needed during their stay at the hospital. This being the case, it was now around 8:00 A.M. during the following morning, when all of a sudden my wife, her father and I were awakened by what sounded like very loud and beautiful choir music echoing right down through the vent next to us. It was a sound that none of us had ever heard before; it consisted of a mixture of high and low tones that were all singing in unison and in a language that none of us had ever heard before either.

Right after this, my wife, my father-in-law and I went back upstairs to where her mother was staying and found out that she had just passed away at exactly 8:00 A.M. We then all looked at each other and realized that what we heard downstairs that very morning was the singing of an angelic choir, which occurred when the gates of Heaven were opened and my wife's mother Conchita was taken back home to be with Jesus in heaven at that very moment. In regards to angelic singing and to prove that what we all heard does indeed exist, the Bible says in Luke 2:12 that "At once the angel was joined by a huge angelic choir singing God's praises." It also says in Luke 2:15: "As the angel choir withdrew into heaven, the sheepherders talked it over. 'Let's get over to Bethlehem as fast as we can and see for ourselves what God has revealed to us". My wife, her father and I were very sad at first, due to the loss of a loved one, but at the same time we were all filled with a great peace in our hearts and minds that was given to us by Jesus himself. This was because we all knew that Conchita Garcia de Yerena had indeed gone home during that morning in June 1988, in order to receive her reward in Heaven and to live with Jesus forever and ever more.

"But for to me, to live is Christ and to die is gain" (Philippians 1:22). Amen! Finally, see the following picture that depicts Jesus himself welcoming my wife Marcia's mother Conchita Garcia de Yerena safely home to Heaven, and also please read the following Lyrics to one of Conchita's favorite songs.

# Welcome Home

# Lyrics to Song #1
# When the Roll is Called Up Yonder

When the trumpet of the Lord shall sound and time shall be
no more,
And the morning breaks, eternal, bright and fair;
When the saved of earth shall gather over on the other shore
And the roll is called up yonder, I'll be there.

When the roll, is called up yon-der,
When the roll, is called up yon-der,
When the roll, is called up yon-der,
When the roll is called up yonder I'll be there.

On that bright and cloudless morning when the dead in Christ
shall rise,
And the glory of His resurrection share;
When His chosen ones shall gather to their home beyond
the skies,
And the roll is called up yonder, I'll be there.

When the roll, is called up yon-der,
When the roll, is called up yon-der,
When the roll, is called up yon-der,
When the roll is called up yonder I'll be there.

Let us labor for the Master from the dawn till setting sun,
Let us talk of all His wondrous love and care;
Then when all of life is over, and our work on earth is done,
And the roll is called up yonder, I'll be there.

When the roll, is called up yon-der,
When the roll, is called up yon-der,
When the roll, is called up yon-der,
**When the roll is called up yonder I'll be there.**

# Chapter 8

# The Soul of a Lost Man

*I*t was in the early morning hours on a Saturday during the summer of 1997 that I had experienced something very hard to explain. It was a bright and beautiful, sunny day. On this particular day I went to take the garbage out as usual when I saw my next door neighbor working in his back-yard. Since I would always stop to say hello to this particular neighbor of mine whenever I saw him, I of course jumped at the opportunity to do so once again. As I began to return to my house, I approached my neighbor before I went inside and we talked for at least a half hour or so before finally finishing our conversation. At the moment that I told this friend of mine I would talk to him later, I then started to walk back towards the rear entrance of my house. At the same moment we each started to walk towards our own homes, I suddenly looked back at my neighbor and noticed that he turned his head clockwise toward his home first, then the rest of his body followed. At the very moment that he did this, I saw what appeared to be a very dark, grayish-colored exact replica of the entire upper portion of his body momentarily trying to leave or slightly protrude outward from his actual body. It was as if his physical body and face had actually moved to the right and his spirit or soul moved outside of his body in the opposite direction to the left.

After a few moments had passed, his spirit somehow began the process of re-connecting itself and in doing so, finally caught up and started to go back inside the upper portion of this man's body. From what I observed, his spirit had the same features as his physical body in every way, shape and form. The only difference was that the coloration of what I saw in regards to his spirit or soul, especially the upper portion of his body that included his face, consisted of a very dark grayish color that did not exist in this world of ours. I also noticed that although his eyes, eyebrows, nose, hair, ears and mouth were all located in the same place as his physical body, I could not see any retinas within his eyes, but instead all I could see was a very blackish type of color. I also saw it within the areas where his eyes, nose and mouth were, which consisted of a greater type of darkness than the other dark-greyish colored areas that covered the rest of his face. After I observed this, it reminded me of what I explained in chapter two of this book, in regards to the coloration of the same facial features of the angel from hell that I saw and the darkness that I saw which covered this angel and the tunnel where it had been standing.

At that moment, I also began to understand that the reason his spirit or soul consisted of a very dark or grayish color was because his soul was lost and without hope; my neighbor did not know yet know Jesus at this time. In regards to the souls of men in general, the Bible says in Christ's account of the rich man and Lazarus (we have the matter summed up and settled) that the soul is indeed conscious after death. In this case, both men died and were buried. Though their bodies were in the graves, each of them was alive and conscious. The rich man in Hell could see, hear, speak and feel. This can be seen in Luke 16:19-31.

There was a rich man who was dressed in purple and fine linen and lived in luxury every day. At his gate was laid a beggar named Lazarus, covered with sores and longing to eat what fell from the rich man's table. Even the dogs came and licked his sores. The time came when the beggar died and the angels carried him to Abraham's side. The rich man also died and was buried. In Hades, where he was in torment, he looked up and saw Abraham far away, with Lazarus by his side. So he called to him, "Father Abraham, have pity on me and send Lazarus to dip the tip of his finger in water and cool my tongue, because I am in agony in this fire." But Abraham replied, "Son, remember that in your lifetime you received your good things, while Lazarus received bad things, but now he is comforted here and you are in agony.

And besides all this, between us and you a great chasm has been set in place, so that those who want to go from here to you cannot, nor can anyone cross over from there to us." He answered, "Then I beg you, father, send Lazarus to my family, for I have five brothers. Let him warn them, so that they will not also come to this place of torment." Abraham replied, "They have Moses and the Prophets; let them listen to them." "No, father Abraham," he said, "but if someone from the dead goes to them, they will repent." He said to him, "If they do not listen to Moses and the Prophets, they will not be convinced even if someone rises from the dead."

As in my neighbor's case, the soul of a man is very real and there is indeed life after death. The unsaved and the saved will be separated from each other. The lost will doubtless carry with them all of the memories that they had of the past and their retribution for rejecting Christ will be endless and be forever. However, the believer can take courage and be comforted. When we move out of this tabernacle of ours, the real man or soul that is saved will leave the body and enter into the presence of the Lord. In regards to my neighbor and what I saw, I am still praying for him every single day, as well as talking to him about God's love and how Jesus was crucified on the cross and rose again so that we could be forgiven of our sins. In doing so, it is my hope that he will soon ask Jesus into his heart and be given the gift of eternal life that will secure a place for him in heaven one day. In addition, I guess I did also realize one more thing from this experience as well and that is when people ask Jesus into their hearts, their souls are also transformed at that very moment. They become pure, or whiter than white, like the color of lightning only even brighter (refer to chapters three and ten).

However, the soul of a lost man is dead, has no life and the coloration is that of the darkest of dark colors since the person has no hope and is headed for an eternity in hell unless they change their minds and ask Jesus into their hearts during this life (refer to chapter two). The good thing though, is that God will never give up on man, even to the very end. Where one chooses to spend eternity will eventually be decided by that very person. Lastly, please see the following picture; even though it cannot depict or describe exactly what I viewed that day, it resembles what I experienced when I saw the upper part of my neighbor's soul momentarily try to leave his physical body, even if only for a very brief period of time.

# The Soul of a lost Man

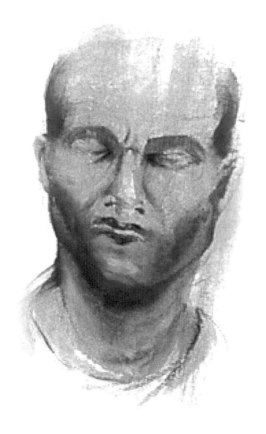

# Chapter 9

# The Crystal Wall from Heaven

*During* the time that I experienced this particular vision, around October of 1977, I was still living in the town of Rice Lake, Wisconsin. It was during this year that I began to develop an even closer relationship with the Lord. I would get up around 4:00 A.M. every morning and spend at least 2 hours in prayer, Bible study and worship. In regards to where I would spend this time with the Lord, it was always on the second floor of the house that I lived in. I would sit in a big sofa that was located near a balcony. The sofa was situated in the corner of a very large living room with only a couple of other pieces of furniture sitting in the other corners. There were also about four or five large windows that were jotted around the upstairs area where I sat. It was sometime during the month of October 1977 that I got up as usual at 4:00 A.M. and looked forward to the quality time that I would be spending with Jesus. However, on this particular day, I spent about an hour in prayer and worship and about a half hour studying the Bible. I then began to sing as well as worship the Lord for around another half hour or so after that. Although I did not know the exact time that I saw this vision, I do believe it was somewhere around 6:00A.M. This was because the sun had not yet risen, but was just beginning to grow lighter outside.

As I closed my eyes again, returning to a state of deep prayer, I then slowly opened my eyes and looked across the room, focusing my eyes towards the north side. As I did this, I was engulfed in perfect peace and although I cannot describe what I saw in all its perfection and detail, I will do the best I can to give a good idea as to the vision that I saw during that time. Upon opening my eyes, I observed what appeared to be a crystal wall that was mostly transparent and had some type of whitish color to it. The wall itself appeared to come down through the ceiling, went down through the floors and also went through each side of the house. It was as if this wall had no beginning or end. The wall, however, did have some type of thickness to it. By this I mean that it appeared to have been around two or three feet thick even though, as said before, it had no beginning or end. As I sat in my chair and continued to observe this crystal wall, I noticed a very small, round blackish entity floating around 3 feet above the floor on the other side of the wall. It began to move toward the outside of the wall. As I focused all of my attention on both the crystal wall and the entity hovering outside of the wall, I realized that what I was observing was actually some type of demon from hell.

Now this particular demon appeared to be about one foot long and six or so inches wide, oblong in shape, as well as had a shade of black that consisted of a darkness that is hard to describe and does not exist in this world of ours as we know it (refer back to chapter two). I did not see any eyes, mouth, nose, or ears on this entity as well. As the demon began to move toward the outside of the crystal wall, it started to squirt from its body or shape in a circular motion what appeared to be a long, black substance toward the wall itself. As the substance made contact with the wall, it was not able to penetrate the wall, but rather started to disintegrate or disappear before it was able to enter into the wall. As the demon itself then tried to enter the crystal wall, it was not able to, but instead began at that time to slowly disintegrate or disappear as well. After this occurred, I watched the crystal wall for a while longer until it slowly disappeared from my sight. In regards to the crystal wall that I saw, I realize that God has provided a wall of protection to all of his children. He has provided a wall that surrounds all who love him on all four sides.

This can also be seen in the scriptures; the devil complained that God had put a wall of protection around Job: "You have always put a wall of protection around him and his home and his property. You have made him prosper in everything he does. Look how rich he is!" (Job 1:10). In regards to the demon that I saw on the outside of the wall that was trying to shoot the black substance at me through the wall itself, the apostle Paul says: "above all, taking the shield of faith, with which you can quench all the flaming darts of the evil one" (Ephesians 6:16, ESV). In addition, to help us stand up to the flaming darts from the Devil, the Apostle Paul says in Ephesians 6:10-18:

> Finally my brethren, be strong in the Lord and in the power of his might; Put on the whole armor of God, that ye may be able to stand against the wiles of the devil; for we wrestle not against flesh and blood, but against principalities, against powers, against the rulers of the darkness of this world, against spiritual wickedness in high places; wherefore take unto you the whole armor of God, that ye may be able to withstand in the evil day, and having done all, to stand; Stand therefore, having your loins girt about with truth, and having on the breastplate of righteousness; and your feet shod with the preparation of the gospel of peace; above all, taking the shield of faith, wherewith ye shall be able to quench all the fiery darts of the wicked; and take the helmet of salvation, and the sword of the Spirit, which is the word of God: praying

always with all prayer and supplication in the Spirit, and watching thereunto with all perseverance and supplication for all saints.

By putting on the whole armor of God we can persevere and win in the fight against darkness and the force of evil itself. In regards to the vision that I saw that day, I have included a picture of the crystal wall from Heaven that I saw, but the wall was thicker, transparent and more whitish in color. You could not see where it began, ended or even stopped. I have also included a picture of what the demon from Hell I saw sort of looked like, which tried to enter the interior portion of the wall itself.

# The Crystal Wall from Heaven

Crystal Wall

Demon

# Chapter 10

# Safely Home

$\mathcal{M}$y father-in-law Celso Yerena, Sr. and I spent many years together and became very close to each other as time went by. Although during this time he spoke mostly Spanish and I mostly English, we managed to communicate to each other with the help of our Lord and through the great love and respect we both had developed for each other. It was around 1996 when we found out that he had developed congestive heart failure, upon being admitted to the emergency room at one of the hospitals near where we live. In spite of this – his medication regime, the difficulties that he faced each day in regards to his health condition and all of the appointments with the many types of doctors he had to see for treatment after his release from the hospital – he continued to serve the Lord with all his heart in how he lived his life with each day. He was not a rich man at all by earthly standards; in fact there were times that he carried little, if any, money in his pocket. However, his riches were not based upon how much he had; it was how he acted and treated each individual that he met which revealed that the riches he had were in his heart, and given to him by the love he had for our Lord and Savior Jesus Christ.

You see, my father-in-law was the kind of person who

brought constant joy into the lives of others wherever he went, whether to a stranger on the street, to the staff in a doctor's office or to the employees of a business, a grocery store or even those who worked within a pharmacy. He would always greet everyone with a big smile and a positive comment, so as to bring a joy to everyone he met and in doing so, brighten up their day. He was also the kind of person who, while at church, would say loudly and without embarrassment, "Gloria a Dios" (or "Glory to God") in order to proclaim the great love he had for the Lord. Yes, he was the type of person whom you would enjoy being around and not only would the qualities of his life begin to change one's own for the better, you would also become that much wiser each time you would talk to or spend time with him on any given day. As the years passed by and as his health continued to decline, he once again ended up back in the hospital, but this time it was the result of a very severe heart attack that he happened to experience on the very day he was admitted to the hospital.

As we all gathered at the hospital on the day that he was admitted during the spring of 1995, the doctors told us that he was not going to make it and even showed us medical proof that he was now considered to be brain dead with little chance for survival. The doctors at the hospital even suggested that we give them permission to remove the oxygen that was helping his body to stay alive. It was then, once we were all informed of the news in regards to his medical condition that we all started to pray. Against all odds we waited throughout the night until early the next morning, believing all the time for a miracle to take place. As the night passed by, morning soon came that next day and along with it, a miracle as well. The miracle I speak of was what had taken place during the night; the doctors informed us all that he was now very much alive and doing well. In addition, the staff at the hospital told us that he had come out of a coma early that morning, was no longer considered to be brain dead and the exams that he was given showed that he now had normal brain activity.

Of course, he had to still stay in the hospital for about a week after that in order to recuperate. He needed to regain his strength until he was given the medical clearance to be released and until we were able to finally bring him back home. On my father-in-law's arrival to his house and after he continued to rest for a few more days, he asked that we all come to see him because he wanted to tell everyone what actually had happened in the hospital. As we all gathered around his bed where he was resting, he informed us that while he was in the hospital, brain dead, in a coma and being kept alive by oxygen, his soul was indeed awake and very much alive within his body. Because of this and according to what he told us, he saw Jesus come into his room and stand right by the very end of his bed. He told us that Jesus spoke to him of many things that were yet to come, that we were living in the last days before his return, that it was not time yet for him to go to his new home in heaven, and that he still had some work to do here on this earth before he would be called back to his heavenly home. He went on to say that Jesus was radiant in color like the color of snow and that his eyes were like lighting or beams of light.

He also told us that Jesus was wearing a long, white robe with a golden garment or belt wrapped around his waist. His hair was shoulder length, parted in the middle, a little curly on both sides and appeared to consist of a mixture of brown as well as light brown colors. His beard was medium in length and he was tall and slender. As soon as Jesus finished speaking to him, Celso went on to tell us that he then saw his wife Conchita who had passed away around 10 years earlier in 1988. According to Celso Sr. she was very beautiful, wore a very whitish colored robe and her face and eyes radiated with an immense glowing white coloration that reflected a peace and love beyond description (refer to chapter three). Apparently, during the visitation he had with his wife Conchita, she told him that it was not time for him to go to heaven yet, even though he wanted to go. She went on to tell him that he still had some work to do here on earth and that Jesus needed him to take care of, as well as spend some more time with, his sons and daughters before he would be called back to Heaven to be with her and most of all, Jesus himself. Well as time went on, my father-in-law did indeed spend even more time with his sons and daughters. He also lived each day as if it were his last and never forgot to tell others how much Jesus loved them as well.

It was around three years later, toward the later part of April 1998 that my father-in-law's health once again took a turn for the worst. He wound up back in the hospital again and when he was released, the doctors told us that he did not have that much more time to live. We continued to spend as much time with him as possible with each day from then on. Unbeknownst to us, it was during May 1998 that Jesus would soon be calling Celso Yerena, Sr. safely back home to be with him and to receive his crown. He would also soon be called back to see as well as be with his loving wife Conchita to walk down the streets of gold in heaven with her forever more. Before this was to happen, however, Jesus still had a few more things that he wanted Celso, Sr. to take care of with the time that he still had remaining on this earth. This included asking all his children to come over to his house so that he could see and talk to each and every one of them. In fact, I remember that very day during the month of May 1998, when he called his sons as well as daughters and I over to his house for a time of sharing and a barbecue. As I recall, on this particular day, he was staring at all of his children as if it was the very first time that he seen them. He then turned to me and said, "Do you know what, my son?"

I replied, "No, what?" He then went on to say with a big smile and a face full of peace that he was very, very happy. After a few weeks had passed, Mother's Day soon arrived on a Sunday during the month of May, 1998. It was on this particular day that my father-in-law woke up early that morning and went out to the store to buy his daughter, my wife, Marcia the most beautiful flowers that you could ever imagine. As he brought them over to our house on that very same day in the afternoon, he then proceeded to give us all a very big hug, went on to then tell us how much he loved us and as always, said, "God bless you" before he returned to his home! Around 6:00 P.M. that same day, my father-in-law called us at our house on the phone. As he was talking to each one of us, he shared with us just how much he loved us, and also went on to say that not only was he at peace with Jesus, but that he would soon be called back to his heavenly home. He then went on to say before he finally hung up the phone, "Dios te bendiga," which means "God bless you" before he finally let us all go. As soon as we got off the phone with my father-in-law, we started our way towards evening worship services at church, but right before we arrived, my wife felt that we should all go back to her father's house to make sure that he was okay. We then headed back to his house and knocked on the door, but because there was no answer, I had to force the door open as a last resort.

As soon as we entered the house, my wife, my daughters and I saw Celso, Sr. lying down on his back on the kitchen floor, with his hands folded to each side and with an expression on his face of pure peace and happiness. We immediately called the ambulance while we all rushed to his side and in doing so, I checked for his pulse, but he had none by that time. As we all kneeled down next to him while holding his hands and overcome with sadness because of our loss, we were also engulfed with a great peace at the same time, because we knew in our hearts where he had gone and we also knew that his work for Jesus here on earth was finally done. Yes, my father-in-law Celso, Sr. lived for Jesus all of his life; he served him faithfully with all of his heart even to the very end. Because of this, he had gone now to claim his crown of glory and to live forever with Jesus, his wife Conchita and all the saints in his new home in Heaven forevermore.

"As for me, I am already being poured out as a libation, and the time of my departure has come. I have fought the good fight, I have finished the race, I have kept the faith. From now on there is reserved for me the crown of righteousness, which the Lord, the righteous judge, will give to me on that day, and not only to me but also to all who have longed for his appearing" (2 Timothy 4:6-8, NRSV). Amen and amen. Finally, please see the following picture that depicts our new home in Heaven and also the lyrics to one of my father-in-laws favorite songs, "Beyond the Sun."

# Our new home in Heaven

## Lyrics to Song #2 – Beyond the Sun

Beyond the sun Even though in this life
I lack wealth
I know that at a place called Glory
I have my mansion
A soul lost
In poverty
Jesus Christ had mercy
On me beyond the sun
Beyond the sun
I have a home, a home
A beautiful home
Beyond the sun like this I go walking
Across the world
Many tests surround me
And there's temptation too
But Jesus Christ
Who is testing me
Will lead me safely
To his mansion beyond the sun
Beyond the sun
I have a home, a home
A beautiful home
Beyond the sun to each of the races
Of human lineage, Christ
Can grant
Complete salvation
And a beautiful house
Made by his own hands has
Been prepared at saint
Zion, for them
Beyond the sun
Beyond the sun
I have a home, a home
A beautiful home

# Chapter 11

# Words of Encouragement and Hope

_Finally_, here we are together at the end of this book, after reading about some of the many true life experiences that others as well as I myself have had, in regards to visions, true stories of the hope and most of all, about God's gift of eternal life that we all can have through his one and only son Jesus Christ our Lord. You now understand after reading this book and most importantly, the many passages of scripture from the Bible that were also included within it, that there really is a Heaven and Hell, that Jesus, the Holy Spirit, Angel's, Demon's and the Devil are not made up, but really do exist, and that man does indeed have a soul that will feel and live forever once a person's body ceases to exist in this world of ours as we know it. Lastly, man by his free choice will decide where he or she spends the rest of eternity, whether in Heaven or Hell. The hope that we all have though, is that in spite of the suffering that we sometimes are faced with and go through as we all pass through this Earth, Jesus will always be there to help those who call upon his precious name. If they chose to do so, they will never ever be forsaken or let go, even until the end of time as we know it.

This can be seen in the following scriptures from the Bible:

"Be strong and of a good courage, fear not, nor be afraid of them: for the LORD thy God, he it is that doth go with thee; he will not fail thee, nor forsake thee" (Deuteronomy 31:6, KJV). "And the LORD, he it is that doth go before thee; he will be with thee, he will not fail thee, neither forsake thee: fear not, neither be dismayed" (Deuteronomy 31:8, KJV). "There shall not any man be able to stand before thee all the days of thy life: as I was with Moses, so I will be with thee: I will not fail thee, nor forsake thee" (Joshua 1:5, KJV). The most important hope we have however, is that of eternal life which Jesus has given to freely to all who ask, which can be seen in the following scriptures.

**The Bible says there is only one way to Heaven.**

Jesus said: "I am the way, the truth, and the life: no man cometh unto the Father but by me" (John 14:6, NKJV).

**Good works cannot save you.**
"For by grace are ye saved through faith; and that not of yourselves: it is the gift of God: Not of works, lest any man should boast" (Ephesians 2:8- 9, KJV).

**Trust Jesus Christ today! Here's what you must do:**

1. **Admit you are a sinner.** "For all have sinned, and come short of the glory of God" (Romans 3:23, KJV). "Wherefore, as by one man sin entered into the world, and death by sin; and so death passed upon all men, for that all have sinned" (Romans 5:12, KJV). "If we say that we have not sinned, we make him a liar, and his word is not in us" (1 John 1:10, KJV).
2. **Be willing to turn from sin (repent).** Jesus said: "I tell you, Nay: but, except ye repent, ye shall all like-wise perish" (Luke 13:5, KJV). "And the times of this

ignorance God winked at; but now commandeth all men everywhere to repent" (Acts 17:30, KJV).

3. **Believe that Jesus Christ died for you, was buried, and rose from the dead.** "For God so loved the world, that he gave his only begotten Son, that whosoever believeth in him should not perish, but have everlasting life" (John 3:16, NIV). "But God commendeth his love toward us, in that, while we were yet sinners. Christ died for us" (Romans 5:8, KJV)."That if thou shalt confess with thy mouth the Lord Jesus, and shalt believe in thine heart that God hath raised him from the dead, thou shalt be saved." (Romans 10:9, KJV).

4. **Through prayer, invite Jesus into your life to become your personal Savior.** "For with the heart man believeth unto righteousness; and with the mouth confession is made unto salvation" (Romans 10:10, KJV). "For whosoever shall call upon the name of the Lord shall be saved" (Romans 10:13, NJKV).

**What to pray:** Dear God, I am a sinner and need forgiveness. I believe that Jesus Christ shed His **precious blood** and died for my sin. I am willing to turn from sin. I now invite Christ to come into my heart and life as my personal Savior.

"But as many as received him, to them gave he the power to become sons of God, even to them that believe on his name" (John 1:12, KJV). "Therefore if any man be in Christ, he is a new creature: old things are passed away; behold, all things are become new" (2 Corinthians 5:17, KJV).

**If you have received Jesus Christ as your Savior, as a Christian you should:**

1. **Read your Bible every day to get to know Christ better.** "Study to show thyself approved unto God, a workman that needeth not to be ashamed, rightly dividing the word of truth" (2 Timothy 2:15, KJV). "Thy word is a lamp unto my feet, and a light unto my path" (Psalm 119:105, KJV).

2. **Talk to God in prayer every day.** "And all things, whatsoever ye shall ask in prayer, believing, ye shall receive" (Matthew 21:22, KJV). "Be careful for nothing; but in everything by prayer and supplication with thanksgiving let your requests be made known unto God" (Philippians 4:6, KJV).

3. **Be baptized, worship, fellowship and serve with other Christians in a church where Christ is preached and the Bible is the final authority.** "Go ye therefore, and teach all nations, baptizing them in the name of the Father, and of the Son, and of the Holy Ghost" (Matthew 28:19, KJV). "Not forsaking the assembling of ourselves together, as the manner of some is; but exhorting one another: and so much the more, as ye see the day approaching" (Hebrews 10:25, KJV). "All scripture is given by inspiration of God, and is profitable for doctrine, for reproof, for correction, for instruction in righteousness" (2 Timothy 3:16, KJV).

4. **Tell others about Christ.** "And he said unto them, Go ye into all the world, and preach the gospel to every creature" (Mark 16:15, KJV). "For though I preach the gospel, I have nothing to glory of: for necessity is laid upon me; yea, woe is unto me, if I preach not the gospel!" (1 Corinthians 9:16, KJV). "For I am not

ashamed of the gospel of Christ: for it is the power of God unto salvation to everyone that believeth; to the Jew first, and also to the Greek" (Romans 1:16, KJV).

When all is said and done then, if anyone does ask Jesus into their hearts, they do indeed have great hope for tomorrow and an eternity of endless joy that awaits them if Jesus should come for them during the rapture, or when they go to be with him in Heaven if they are still on this earth when their bodies pass away. In closing then, I pray that you were blessed as well as touched in a special way by this book, that it has strengthened your faith and either saved you or brought you closer to Jesus our Lord and Savior. I also hope and pray that you, too, have or will become fishers of men's souls for Jesus. If this is the case, then I will know that my purpose for writing this book has not been in vain and that Jesus has indeed been glorified in the creation and publication of it as well. Lastly, before you go, please view the following Bible scriptures as well as picture, which I pray will not only be a blessing to you, but also encourage you as much as they have encouraged me:

**"Thou shalt guide me with thy counsel, and afterward receive me to glory" Psalm 73:24.**

All of life is here summed up in one verse. "While I am here on this earth," the psalmist prays to the Lord, "You will *guide me.*" You will give me the direction I need for each step of the way. You will never leave me or forsake me. You will help me when I stumble and you will steer me when I lose my way. What's more, you will guide me *with thy counsel.* This is no mere human, fallible leader. You are an all-knowing, all-wise escort. You will never give me wrong advice or send me in a wrong direction. I will never meet a problem for which you do not know the solution and I will never get so off course that you cannot guide me back to safety. However, that is all just life on earth! Afterward, you will *receive me to glory*. After you have carefully and lovingly directed my way here, you will usher me into your glorious presence in heaven. There is no intermediary state – death is not a tunnel, it is a door. When you release my hand in this world, you will receive me into the next. There is no "sending"; there is only *guiding* and then *receiving* – no time apart from you. Death, where is your sting? Grave, where is your victory? Devil, where is your terror? **My God will guide me with His counsel and then receive me to His glory.**

## Isaiah 51:3

[3] For the LORD will comfort Zion, He will comfort all her waste places; He will make her wilderness like Eden, And her desert like the garden of the LORD; Joy and gladness will be found in it, Thanksgiving and the voice of melody (NKJV).

**Never Alone**

CPSIA information can be obtained at www.ICGtesting.com
Printed in the USA
LVOW01s1336211213

366324LV00003B/168/P

9 781624 198267